VIKINGS

CHELSEA HOUSE
PUBLISHERS
A Haights Cross Communications Company ®
www.chelseahouse.com

First hardcover library edition published in the United States of America in 2006 by Chelsea House Publishers, a subsidiary of Haights Cross Communications. All rights reserved.

A Haights Cross Communications ✦ Company ®

www.chelseahouse.com

Library of Congress Cataloging-in-Publication
Gassos, Dolores.
  Vikings / Dolores Gassos.
    p. cm. — (Ancient civlizations)
  Includes bibliographical references and index.
  ISBN 0-7910-8490-6 (hard cover)
  1. Vikings—Juvenile literature. 2. Civilization, Viking—Juvenile literature. I. Title. II. Ancient civilizations (Philadelphia, Pa.)
  DL65.G37 2006
  948'.022—dc22

                        2005012561

Production and Realization
Parramón Ediciones, S.A.

Text
Dolores Gassós

Translator
Patrick Clark

Illustrations
Marcel Socias Studio

Graphic Design and Typesetting
Estudi Toni Inglés (Alba Marco)

First edition: April 2005

Ancient Civilizations
Vikings

Printed in Spain
© Parramón Ediciones, S.A. – 2005
Ronda de Sant Pere, 5, 4ª planta
08010 Barcelona (España)
Empresa del Grupo Editorial Norma

www.parramon.com

TABLE OF CONTENTS

A PEOPLE WITHOUT FRONTIERS

The Vikings were a bold and experienced seafaring people who kept all of the coasts of Europe on edge for two centuries with their incursions in search of land and riches. They were also good merchants, and were the first European group to set off on long voyages of geographical discovery. The most important part of their legacy is maintained in Scandinavian countries. Looking beyond their areas of origin, the most important lesson the Vikings left was in their ability to achieve great deeds with scarce material means, relying, above all, on courage and strength.

This book aims to awaken in young readers an interest in the history and reality of the Vikings through a brief introduction, and a discussion of 11 topics that cover the most important aspects of a culture that set the stage for the Middle Ages in Europe. The central image of each double page gives an immediate impression about the topic under discussion, while the texts, which are informative and anecdotal at the same time, present basic knowledge about the subject at hand. At the end of the book, there is a chronology of the principal milestones of Viking history, and a small list of interesting facts.

THE TERROR OF THE SEAS

The bow decoration of the Viking *drakkars* was very sophisticated.

SEAFARING PEOPLE OF THE NORTH

The Vikings were a seafaring people who lived in the territories occupied today by Denmark, the southern part of Norway, and the southern part of Sweden, from about the fifth century to the twelfth century. They lived in lands where the winters were harsh and summers were short, where woods and lakes covered most of the territory. The scarcity of available land for farming and the adverse climate made agriculture very difficult. Only a few grains (barley, rye, and hay) and a few vegetables were able to be cultivated. The Vikings had to support themselves by means of activities such as fishing or raising livestock, from which they obtained skins and fat, as well as meat and milk. From the forests, they took the wood they needed to build their houses and also their boats, the famous *drakkars*.

The Vikings lived according to the rhythm of the seasons: in spring and summer they could go out to sea, cultivate the soil, and let their livestock graze in meadows. During the fall and winter, the boats were kept in sheds, the livestock was confined to stables, and men, women, and children spent long evenings huddled next to the fire, playing dice and telling incredible tales of adventure. At this time of year, the Vikings depended on food reserves they had built up during the spring and summer.

VIKING FURY FALLS ON EUROPE

These northern sailors called themselves Vikings, but outside their lands they were called Normans, which means "men from the North." In their first expeditions, far from their areas of origin, the Normans, or Vikings, sought areas rich in fishing and deserted or sparsely populated lands that they could colonize.

Europe in the time of the Vikings.

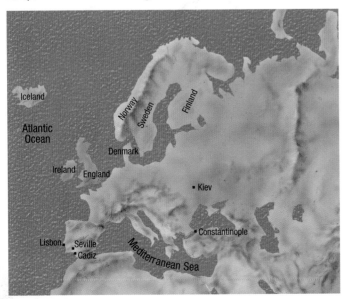

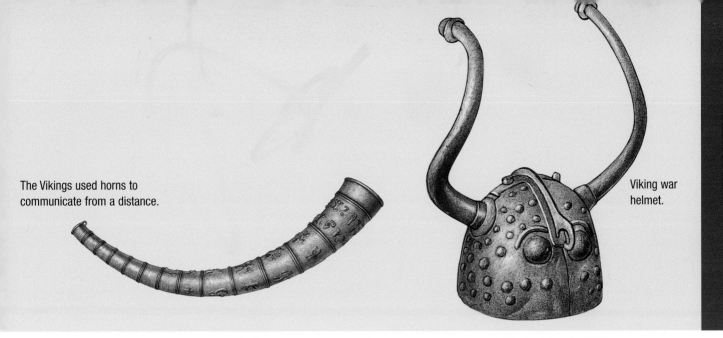

The Vikings used horns to communicate from a distance.

Viking war helmet.

They were basically a peaceful people, until they attacked the Lindisfarne monastery in England in the year 793. After that, their attacks on the European coasts were repeated with macabre regularity every spring and summer until the year 1100, a date that marks the end of the so-called Viking era.

Once they realized how easy it was to obtain riches from sacking a monastery, the Vikings decided to resort to this method to provide themselves with the materials they lacked, such as metals, and set out more and more often for Southern Europe. After planting the seeds of terror in Holland and France, where they were responsible for a large-scale massacre in the city of Nantes, they arrived as far as Galicia, where they created a wave of destruction on the coastlines. Then they went to Lisbon, Cadiz, and Seville, a city they sacked in 844. A few months later, it was on to Paris, where they returned from time to time. Viking ships, in addition to being able to cross the seas, could enter into river channels in order to arrive in the very heart of Europe.

FROM PILLAGERS TO KINGS

In order to put a stop to attacks by these fearsome warriors, several European kings made peace with them and ceded them territory. The first to do so was Alfred the Great of England. In the year 911, Charles III ("the Simple") of France gave the Viking Rollon some lands on the northern coast of France. This area came to be called Normandy, because it was populated by Normans, or Vikings, and it constituted a hereditary duchy, of which Rollon was the first duke.

This event marked the beginning of a period of expansion outside their lands of origin. It is believed that one of the major reasons for Viking expeditions was to seek new space for the settlement of an ever-increasing population that could subsist only with great difficulty in the cold lands to the north. The Vikings settled in various areas of England and Ireland, in the French area of Normandy, and even on the island of Sicily. In some areas, they came to establish important kingdoms, such as those ruled by Canute the Great, William the Conqueror, and Roger II of Sicily, and they left enduring traces of their cultural heritage in these places.

Bronze figure
of the god Frey.

MERCHANTS WHO TRAVELED EAST

The most ferocious and bloodthirsty Vikings were those who lived in Denmark. Their most famous kings, Sven I (986–1014) and Canute I, the Great (1016–1035), created an empire that included Denmark, England, and Norway, but this kingdom lasted only a short time.

The Vikings of Norway began by colonizing the islands located to the west and north of their lands, and thus arrived on the shores of Iceland. In the year 981, Eric the Red ventured as far as Greenland, and there is documented evidence that his sons Leif and Thorvald landed in a place they called Vinland ("land of vines"), which is usually identified with Nova Scotia. The Vikings of Norway began their pillaging in the year 795, when they first attacked and then colonized the coasts of Ireland.

The Swedish Vikings, called Varegs or Rus, were more interested in trade than pillaging, and their expeditions in search of places to exchange their wares followed the course of the Volga and Dnieper rivers. They arrived as far as Constantinople, a city they harassed on several occasions, thereby obliging the emperor of Byzantium to cede them important commercial advantages. In this manner, the Vikings fulfilled an important role as intermediaries in the trading of goods between the East and the West. In Byzantium and Turkistan, they dealt in slaves, skins, and weapons coming from the West; in England and France, they sold silks and spices brought from the Orient.

Stone tumulus in the shape of a boat.

Re-creation of a *Valkyrie*, a woman warrior from the Viking pantheon.

The Varegs conquered some cities in the areas through which they passed, cities such as Kiev or Novgorod, and made them capitals of a duchy that is considered to be the origin of the Russian State.

CHRISTIANITY ENDS THE VIKING WORLD

While all of these events were happening, the first Christian missionaries began to preach Christianity in the lands of the Vikings. The Vikings were pagans. Their religion was based on a rich mythology that featured a multitude of gods and fabulous creatures, such as elves or forest dwarves. Viking mythology was basically transmitted by oral tradition, but also inspired some texts, written beginning in the twelfth century and still preserved today. Christianity spread rapidly, and soon the first churches were built. In the beginning, these churches were more influenced by Viking art than Christian art.

The Vikings did not construct large buildings, but they reached a considerable level of skill in the decorative arts. They decorated their boats with beautiful sculptures depicting terrifying animal heads, and with geometrically inspired or animal-shaped carvings on the most visible parts of the wood. In addition, the handles and covers of their swords were richly decorated, as were, sometimes, even their shields and helmets. In this way, entwined patterns with stylized drawings of animals were particularly emphasized.

The Viking era came to an end around 1100, when they were defeated in battles, such as that of Clondorf, in Ireland, and when some of their kings converted to Christianity, thereby becoming part of Europe in the Middle Ages.

Silver crucifix from the tenth century (National Museum of Stockholm). This is the oldest image of Christ in Scandinavia.

SAILING AGAINST WINDS AND TIDES

Viking ships, generally called *drakkars*, were the basis for the prosperity of this Northern European people. This type of ship was used for fishing, for trade, and also for attacking other European civilizations, in search of rich booty. Depending on their use, boats could be made stronger, or able to transport more cargo, or lighter, and therefore easier to maneuver. Thanks to the efficacy of these ships, and to their expertise in navigation, the Vikings kept all of Europe on edge for several centuries.

■ tent
at night, if they could not dock on land, crew members made a cloth tent in the center of the boat for shelter

■ chests
each Viking carried his own chest, where he would store his belongings and booty, and where he would sit to ride and to row

■ pillage and trade
ships for pillaging rode high on the water, and could, therefore, maneuver in shallow waters; those used for trade were designed to ride lower, in order to be able to transport heavy merchandise

dimensions ■
Viking ships measured about 80 feet long, 17 feet wide, rose about 6 feet out of the water, and could hold about 23 tons of cargo

stability ■
as a result of their peculiar configuration, *drakkars* were very stable, and could, therefore, navigate the rough seas of the Atlantic Ocean successfully

oars ■
drakkars had a collapsible mast and a rectangular sail, but also had between 20 and 50 oars for use when the occasion arose

TOOLBOX
The Vikings knew how to smelt bronze and forge iron, and, using these materials, they made a great quantity of utensils that they used for building boats and for many other tasks. In 1936, a Viking toolbox containing more than 200 pieces was found in Mästermyr (Sweden).

TOWARD AMERICA

With their fast and safe ships, the Vikings ventured across the Atlantic Ocean, and arrived in Greenland. It is even believed that they landed in Nova Scotia, on the American continent, four centuries before Christopher Columbus arrived on the island of Hispaniola.

■ **sails**
the sails were bound to the mast, and also to the bow and the stern of the ship, which reached a considerable height

drakkar ■
the word *drakkar* means "dragon," and the origin of this term is found in the dragon or terrifying animal figure that was used to adorn the bow of Viking ships

wood ■
drakkars were made of oak, and their construction was carried out with admirable attention to detail and perfectionism

EUROPE TREMBLES BEFORE THE VIKINGS

The Vikings lived in an area of Northern Europe that coincides with the present-day territories of Denmark, the southern end of Norway, and the southern end of Sweden. These lands were not very suitable for agriculture, because of the low fertility of their soils, and especially because of the rigors of extremely cold winters. For this reason, the Vikings chose to seek riches outside of their areas of origin through trade, colonization, and attacks on the wealthiest monasteries and cities in Europe.

British Isles ■
the first pillaging expeditions by the Vikings were launched against rich monasteries in Northern England and Ireland

William the Conqueror ■
in 1066, William the Conqueror, duke of Normandy, conquered the southern end of England, and created a Norman kingdom with himself as king

Normandy ■
in the year 911, the king of France gave the Vikings the territory of Normandy, where they settled and to which they gave its name

Upriver ■
these fierce Nordic warriors not only attacked the coasts, but also went upriver to arrive at cities such as Seville, Antwerp, Toulouse, and Paris

NEW CITIES

The Vikings not only pillaged the coasts of Europe, but also, in some cases, settled there and founded cities. In Ireland, for example, the Vikings founded the cities of Cork and Dublin, the present-day capital of the country.

THE BIRTH OF RUSSIA

Swedish Vikings, or Varegs, founded the kingdom of Kiev, the birthplace of Russia. These origins are echoed in the very name of Russia, which comes from the term Rus, a Slavic name for the Vikings.

■ North Atlantic
as early as the eighth and ninth
centuries, Vikings visited the
Shetland, Orkney, and Faröe
archipelagoes, as well as the
large island of Iceland, where
they settled

■ Eastern Europe
in the East, Vikings sailed
up the Dnieper and Volga
rivers, as far as the
Caspian and Black seas,
where they established
contact with the
Byzantine Empire

■ Southern Europe
little by little, the Viking *drakkars*
ventured further and further south,
and managed to cross the Straits
of Gibraltar to enter the
Mediterranean Sea

■ Italy
in the eleventh century, the
Normans attacked Italy, where they
came to create the Kingdom of Two
Sicilys, composed of the southern
part of the Italian peninsula and the
island of Sicily

THE VIKINGS ARE COMING!

In addition to being expert navigators, the Vikings were also fierce warriors. When the good weather arrived, they organized pillaging expeditions to the coasts of Europe. When the outline of a Viking ship appeared on the horizon, the inhabitants of an area were seized with terror. They tried to escape to safety, and did not return to their homes until the invaders had gone away with their booty.

steering the ships ■
while traveling in their *drakkars*, Viking warriors had to control the sails or row in order to steer the ship

protection ■
the crew entrusted their safety to the dragon on the bow of the ship; the dragon was also supposed to chase away the evil spirits of enemies

information ■
the ships were outlined on the horizon in formations of three or four ships, and watchmen on the coasts raised an alert when they spotted them

the attack ■
once on land, the warriors jumped out of their ships and tried to seize as much loot as possible; if necessary, they killed anyone who stood in their way

Finely decorated weapons

In almost every Viking town, there was a place dedicated to forging iron. There, iron swords were made. The hilts and sheaths of these swords were decorated with great care.

fighting ■
fighting, when it happened, was done with swords and hammer blows, but the enemy often fled and left the battlefield free for pillagers

WITH SHIPS ON THEIR BACKS

When they were sailing on a river and came to a stretch that was not navigable, the Vikings, rather than turn back, brought the boats to shore, put them on wooden boards, and slid them up the valley to a point where the river was again suitable for navigation.

■ **battle**
on occasion, Christian troops stood up to the Vikings, engaging in fierce battles

■ **booty**
once they had gathered a large booty, Viking warriors returned to their *drakkars* and went back out to sea

■ **iron**
gear for attacking and for defense consisted of swords, helmets, and shields of iron. At times, they also used hammers made of this same metal

■ **attire**
warriors wore a tunic tied with a belt, and pants to which they tied the straps of their boots

VILLAGES ON THE SEASHORE

Viking villages were located mainly on the shores of the sea, although there were some in interior regions. This northern people did not live in cities or large towns, but rather in small villages made up of a handful of houses. The same men who performed the deeds of fierce warriors abroad became farmers, ranchers, or fishermen upon return to their homeland, where they led a quiet life based on the rhythm of the seasons.

roofs ■
a roof with two sloping sides was made with wooden sticks, and covered with straw or grasses

■ fishing
fishing was a very important activity for feeding the group; the most prized catch was codfish, which was hung out to dry in the open air

houses ■
houses were rectangular in shape, and generally built with large wooden planks

openings ■
Viking houses had a door on each side and no windows; in the middle of the roof, there was an opening to allow the smoke from cooking to leave the house

livestock ■
raising animals, particularly sheep and goats, brought many useful products, such as meat, milk, and wool

furnishings ■
inside the houses, there were large tables with wooden benches, beds next to the walls, and skins and blankets for protection from the cold

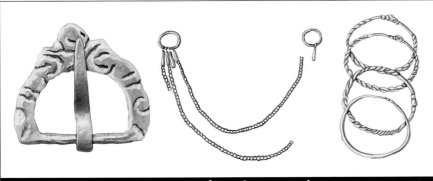

Ornaments of precious metals

The richest Vikings wore beautiful ornaments, such as buckles and brooches of gold and bronze, gold bracelets, and silver earrings and collars.

WEALTH OF THE SEA

In addition to fish, the sea provided the Vikings with seals, walruses, and whales, animals of great abundance, which they hunted in order to make use of their skins, their fat, and their tusks.

hearth ■
because windows were lacking, houses were lit primarily by a fire in the hearth, which also provided heat and was used for cooking food

women's work ■
when the men were away, women took care of all the work that needed to be done, and occupied themselves with knitting tunics and blankets for protection from the cold

agriculture ■
rye and barley, grains that could be used to feed people and livestock, as well as straw, were grown in fields near the village

■ torches
torches or whale oil lamps were lit when needed

STONES WITH INTERESTING MESSAGES

The Vikings did not have a written culture based on books and documents, but rather transmitted their customs and traditions by oral means. Nevertheless, they had an alphabet whose letters are called runes, and Viking writing is therefore known as runic writing. This alphabet appeared some three centuries before the time of the Vikings, but the Vikings were the first to use it to create runic stones. These stones are large monoliths with inscriptions and drawings, and they were usually built in honor of the dead.

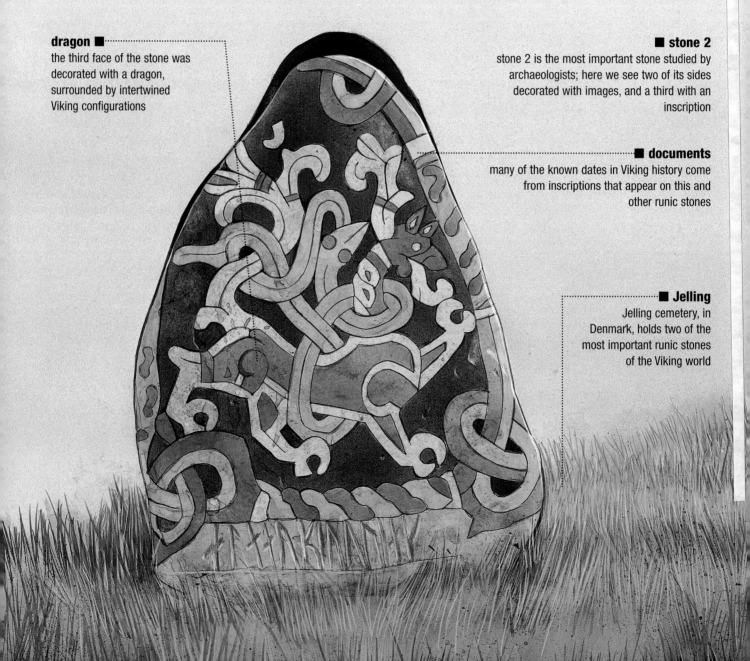

dragon ■
the third face of the stone was decorated with a dragon, surrounded by intertwined Viking configurations

■ stone 2
stone 2 is the most important stone studied by archaeologists; here we see two of its sides decorated with images, and a third with an inscription

■ documents
many of the known dates in Viking history come from inscriptions that appear on this and other runic stones

■ Jelling
Jelling cemetery, in Denmark, holds two of the most important runic stones of the Viking world

The runic alphabet

The first runic alphabet consisted of 24 characters, but was reduced in the Viking era to only 16 symbols. After the arrival of Christianity, it was gradually replaced by the Latin alphabet.

GALLEHUS'S GOLDEN HORN

One of the oldest examples of runic writing is an inscription with the name of the author engraved onto a golden horn found near Gallehus, in Denmark, which dates from around 400 A.D.

■ Jesus Christ
as a tangible sign of his conversion to Christianity, King Harald II had one of the faces of the stone engraved with a figure of the crucified Christ

■ Viking art
the figure of Christ is intertwined with decorative motifs that are typically Viking in style; this was often the case with early Christian art in Nordic countries

■ dedication
according to the inscription, King Harald II ordered the stone to be engraved in memory of his father, Gorm, and his mother, Thorvi

■ proclamation
in addition to honoring his parents, King Harald II makes it known that he has conquered all of Denmark and Norway for himself, and proclaims that he has brought Christianity to the Danes

FORTIFIED PLAZAS FOR DEFENSE

There is no evidence that the Vikings constructed fortified plazas systematically, given that their main enemies, whose coasts they frequented in pillaging raids, were hundreds or even thousands of miles away. They did, however, build a few forts to prepare for pillaging or colonizing expeditions, before setting off for their intended targets. These fortresses were designed according to an existing pattern, making all of their forts similar to each other.

location ■
Viking fortified plazas were often located in areas surrounded by one or more rivers, which served as a natural defense

ditches ■
a large ditch dug in the earth surrounded the entire complex, and a second ditch surrounded the central nucleus of the fortress

fences ■
wooden fences, reinforced with mounds of earth, were built around the central nucleus

The fortified plaza of Fyrcat

in the Danish town of Fyrcat, a Viking fortified plaza dating from the end of the tenth century was excavated; its central ring housed enough buildings to form 12 squares.

administration ■
buildings in the central precincts were generally used for military, administrative, and commercial functions

BUILDINGS SHAPED LIKE SHIPS
The buildings in fortified plazas resemble the shape of Viking ships, which were a symbol of protection and prosperity for this seafaring people.

buildings ■
the buildings, in the style of Viking houses, were arranged to form squares, with a large open space in the center

■ residential zone
the houses that served as residences for warriors, and eventually for their families, were located outside the central precincts

circle ■
the heart of the fortified plaza was generally circular in shape and was divided into four equal parts

■ wood
stone was not used in building these fortified plazas, which were constructed exclusively using wood

THOR, THE GOOD-NATURED GOD OF THUNDER

In the rich Viking mythology, the father of all the gods is Odin, who delivered one of his eyes as payment in order to be able to drink a sip from the fountain of Mimin, and thus acquire wisdom. Odin is the god of war and knowledge, the inventor of runic writing, and of all the arts. He appears in the guise of a one-eyed old man, and wears a long white beard. With his wife, Freya, he started the Aryan race. After Odin, the most important of the Viking gods is his son, Thor, who lives in Asgard, the homeland of the gods, in a mansion with more than 400 rooms and a shining silver roof.

Jormangundr ■
Jormangundr, the sea serpent, was the main enemy of human beings on earth, and Thor finally succeeded in killing her after repeated attempts

death ■
victory over the serpent was a great triumph for Thor, but it cost him his life when the beast poisoned him with her venomous breath

beloved god ■
for having liberated the land of human beings from the threat of Jormangundr, Thor was the most beloved god of the Vikings

The queen of the goddesses

The wife of Odin, called Freya or Frigga, was the goddess of love, marriage, rain, and fertility. She knew the future, but could not reveal it, and she was considered the perfect wife. The English word Friday and the German word Freitag come from her name.

THOR'S HAMMER

According to legend, Thor lost his hammer one day and came to Loki to ask for help in finding it. Loki sent him to the land of the giants, where the hammer was, but Thrym, the king of the giants, asked to marry Freya as a condition for returning the hammer. Then Loki disguised Thor as Freya, and when Thrym was about to seal the marriage with a hammer blow, Thor grabbed the hammer and killed all the giants with it.

■ **appearance**

Thor is a god of mature age who can be recognized by his red beard and wide shoulders

■ **hammer**

his weapon is a hammer called *mejöllnir* ("the destroyer"), which returns automatically to the hands of the person who throws it

■ **glove**

in order to control his powerful hammer, Thor needs to cover his hand with an iron glove

muscles ■

Thor is a warrior god, enemy of the giants, whom he fights tirelessly, and because of this he has very developed muscles and a flat stomach

belt ■

Thor ties his clothes with a magic belt, which doubles his physical strength

FINAL VIKING RESTING PLACE

When a Viking died, his mortal remains were deposited in tombs that also held various objects of daily use or adornments indicating the social position of the deceased. These tombs were located in collective cemeteries, and were marked with stones whose shape indicated whether the people buried were men or women, or whether the people buried there held a distinguished position in society.

chiefs ■
men of high social rank were buried inside a *drakkar*, which was then buried in the cemetery, with its tallest parts sticking out of the ground

chests ■
chests containing objects important to the deceased, including such items as his shields and swords, were placed on both sides of the deathbed

AN INTACT CEMETERY

In Norresundby, in Denmark, there is a perfectly preserved Viking cemetery, located on a hill, over a wide clearing, on which grass is growing.

■ stones

inside the cemeteries were groups of stones cut in different sizes that sketched out different shapes

■ men

stones arranged in the shape of a boat indicated the tombs of men

■ women

graves of women could be recognized by the arrangement of stones in a circle

■ funerary trousseau

the funerary trousseau of an important man could include objects as varied as beds, campaign tents, decorated carts, sleds, looms, or shoes

■ animals

in some cases, animals owned by the deceased, such as horses and dogs, were also buried with him or her

■ clearings

the Vikings usually chose clearings, places devoid of trees, for their cemeteries

■ cadavers

the bodies of distinguished men were placed in the center of a *drakkar*, on a bed

Oseberg

A funerary *drakkar*, with skeletons and a large trousseau, including four carts decorated as the illustration shows, was found in the Norwegian town of Oseberg in 1904.

HELPFUL SERVANTS AND WOMEN WARRIORS

In Viking mythology, the *Valkyries* are women warriors who live in Odin's palace to take care of it as guardians and to serve him food and beverages. In addition, Odin sends them to all the battlefields to decide who should die. The *Valkyries* are known by name (Hlin, Gna, Lofn, Vjofr, Syn…) and each of them has a specific mission, such as carrying the petitions of human beings to the gods.

steeds ■
The *Valkyries* are young damsels, mounted on elegant steeds, who ride through the air

Wagner and the *valkyries*

In the mid-nineteenth century, German composer Richard Wagner wrote *The Ring of the Nibelungs*, a cycle of four operas (*Das Rheingold*, *Die Walküre*, *Siegfried*, and *Die Götterdammerung*), which brings to life fictional characters from Saxon and Scandinavian mythology.

VALHALIA

The Vikings called the paradise where those who obtained the favor of the gods after death were brought by the name of Valhalla. Valhalla was a part of Asgard, the house of the gods, whose walls were made of shields and whose roof was made of lances.

dawn ■
in Viking mythology, it is said
that the lights of dawn are
nothing more than the
reflections of the shields
of the *Valkyries*

■ **wings**
they have full blond heads of
hair that wave in the wind,
and wear a winged helmet
on their head to help them
in their flight

■ *Valkyries*
their name means
"choosers of the fallen,"
because they decide who
must die in each battle

■ **clothes**
their white clothing indicates
their virginity, and their light,
airy clothing is designed to
show their lightness
and agility

bearers ■
the *Valkyries* gather up the heroes who
have fallen in battle and carry them off
to paradise or Valhalla, where they are
received with a drink

■ **warriors**
they are women warriors, and
they carry a lance and shield, and
wear sandals that go up to the
middle of their leg

■ **invisible**
they are invisible to ordinary
mortals; the only people who can
see them are warriors who are
about to die on the battlefield

A VIKING LEGACY

In the tenth century, when Christianity began to spread in Norway, the Vikings were at the height of their splendor. Thus, it is natural that the first Norwegian churches show an appreciation for Viking craftsmanship, above all in ornamental details. These churches are made of wood, and although most of the oldest ones have disappeared, 29 temples of the twelfth century remain to illustrate the symbiotic relationship between the Viking legacy and early Norwegian Christianity.

INTERIORS WITH COLUMNS

Inside, the *stavkirker* usually consisted of a nave and a choir area, with one or more wooden columns in the center to support the high roofs in that part of the church.

■ jambs

on the upper part, the planks of the walls are fastened to a horizontal piece of timber, called a jamb, for roof support

■ multilevel buildings

churches came to have as many as four upper levels, with roofs on each one

■ corner planks

the planks in the corners are twice as wide as normal, and are arranged in an angle

Following the wind

Metal weathervanes decorated in Viking style were placed atop the tallest churches to indicate the direction of the wind.

dragons ■

figures in the shape of a dragon that decorate the top of some roofs resemble those on the bows of Viking *drakkars*

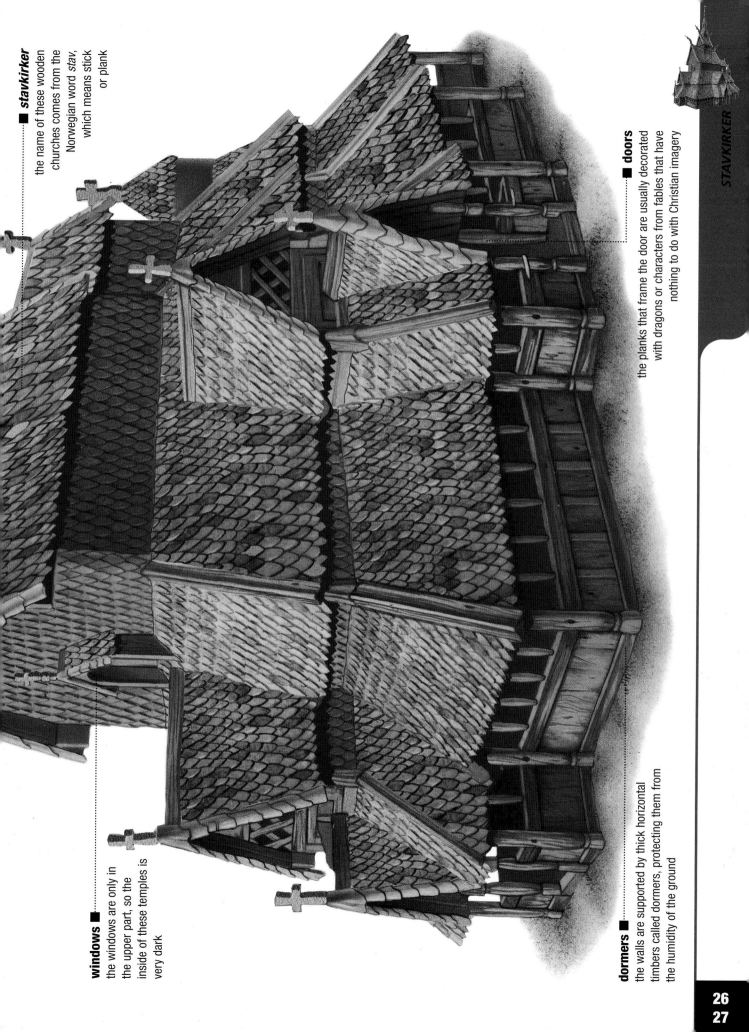

■ *stavkirker*
the name of these wooden churches comes from the Norwegian word *stav*, which means stick or plank

windows ■
the windows are only in the upper part, so the inside of these temples is very dark

dormers ■
the walls are supported by thick horizontal timbers called dormers, protecting them from the humidity of the ground

■ **doors**
the planks that frame the door are usually decorated with dragons or characters from fables that have nothing to do with Christian imagery

WILLIAM THE CONQUEROR, A VIKING KING

William the Conqueror was a descendant of the Vikings who settled in Normandy after the year 911 and created an aristocracy there. He was the illegitimate son of Duke Robert the Devil, but his father recognized him as a legitimate heir, and he became the new Duke of Normandy in 1035. He had to confront a long civil war in his territories, and when his cousin Edward the Confessor, king of England, named William heir to his kingdom, he had to reckon with Count Harold, whom he defeated in the Battle of Hastings.

■ **king of England**
after winning the Battle of Hastings, William the Conqueror was proclaimed king of England, and he held the throne until his death in 1087

KING WILLIAM "THE CONQUEROR"

King William became known as "the Conqueror" for his conquest of England in 1066. From him, came the figure of the *shire*, which is still a name for an English title.

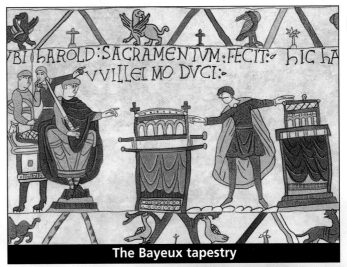

The Bayeux tapestry

The Norman conquest of England is depicted in great detail on the Bayeux tapestry, a cloth measuring 230.77 feet in length by 1.64 feet in width, and bordered by wools in eight colors. Surrounded by a frieze with animals, foliage and hunting scenes, it is kept in the city of Bayeux, in France.

cavalry ■
once on land, the Normans put on their armaments and helmets, and mounted their horses

■ **drakkars**
the *drakkar* boats in which they sailed attested to the Viking origins of the Normans

■ **Pevensey**
the duke's boats traveled from Normandy to Pevensey, in England, where the soldiers disembarked with their horses

■ **Christians**
unlike their Viking ancestors, the Normans of the time of William the Conqueror were Christians, and, for this reason, they carried shields with crosses

■ **toward England**
to defend his claim to the throne of England, William the Conqueror sent his forces toward his neighboring country

■ **tragic end**
after a fierce campaign, the Normans killed Lewine and Gyrd, the brothers of Count Harold

■ **Hastings**
the final defeat of Harold took place at the Battle of Hastings in 1066

CHRONOLOGY

YEARS	HISTORICAL FACTS
793	Pillage of the Lindisfarne monastery, in England.
795	First pillaging expeditions on the Irish coasts.
823	Bishop Ebo of Rheims, the first Christian missionary, arrives in Denmark.
834	Norwegian Vikings begin the occupation of Ireland.
839	Swedish Vikings arrive for the first time in Constantinople.
841	Foundation of Dublin by Norwegian Vikings.
843	Viking attack on the estuary of Garona and of Toulouse.
844	Danish Vikings occupy Cadiz and sack Seville.
845	First sack of Paris.
850	Construction of the first Christian churches in Viking territory.
857	Renewed pillaging of Paris.
859	Danish Vikings attack the northern part of Italy.
860	Sack of Pisa.
862	Swedish Vikings, led by Ruril, take the Slavic city of Novgorod.
866	Swedish Vikings besiege Constantinople.
874	Colonization of Iceland begins.
878–954	Vikings occupy an area of England, which they call Danelaw, or "area Subject to the law of the Danes."
882	The kingdom of Rus begins with the unification of Kiev and Novgorod.
885	Vikings besiege Paris nonstop for a year.
911	Charles III ("the Simple") cedes the territories that would become known as Normandy to the Viking Rollon.
960	Christianization of Denmark following the baptism of Harald II "Blue Tooth."
966	Renewed Viking raids on the Iberian Peninsula.
971	Viking defeat in Galicia at the hands of the troops of Count Gonzalo Sanchez.
985	Beginning of the colonization of Greenland, discovered in 981.
1013	King Sven I of Denmark conquers England and incorporates it into his kingdom.
1014	King Brian Boru of Ireland decisively defeats the Vikings at the Battle of Clonturf.
1035	Canute the Great dies, and the Viking Danish Empire disappears with him.
1066	William the Conqueror wins the Battle of Hastings and conquers England.
1100	Viking raids end for good.
1130	The Normans create the kingdom of Sicily.

DID YOU KNOW... ?

...the word *Viking* comes from an old Nordic word, *vikingr*, meaning "Scandinavian on a pillaging expedition"?

...the word Norman (as the Vikings are also known) was given to them by the Franks, and means "men of the North"?

...their expansion was not only required by the harsh conditions of their native lands, but also by oral traditions, which asked them to leave for distant lands without fear of the unknown?

...they performed human sacrifices, during which they opened the chest cavity of a prisoner, tore out his lungs, and offered them to Odin?

...some of the most popular names among the Vikings were Harald, Sven, Eric, and Olav?

...in the Roskilde Viking Museum (in Denmark), there is a splendid *drakkar* (82 feet long, with room for 32 rowers) in very good condition that was discovered in Gokstad at the end of the nineteenth century?

...the United States sent up two probes to Mars in 1975, both called *Viking*, in honor of this intrepid and exploring people, to find out whether life exists on the Red Planet?

...the names Iceland and Greenland mean "land of ice" and "green country," respectively, and were coined by the Vikings?

...King Olav II Haraldsson of Norway converted to Christianity, was canonized, and is the patron saint of his country?

...the Vikings believed in elves, dwarfs who made weapons for the gods, and who sang and danced in the woods in the moonlight?

...the Vikings thought that Earth was made from the skin of Ymir, the evil ice giant, and that the mountains were made from his bones, vegetation from his hair, and cliffs from his teeth?